P9-ARG-287

MEGAN RAPINOE

by Jill Sherman

AMICUS | AMICUS INK

Amicus High Interest and Amicus Ink are published by Amicus
P.O. Box 1329, Mankato, MN 56002
www.amicuspublishing.us

Library of Congress Cataloging-in-Publication Data
Names: Sherman, Jill, author.
Title: Megan Rapinoe / by Jill Sherman.
Description: Mankato, Minnesota : Amicus, Amicus Ink, [2020] | Series: Pro
  sport biographies | Includes index. | Audience: K to Grade 3.
Identifiers: LCCN 2018038007 (print) | LCCN 2018038670 (ebook) | ISBN
  9781681517469 (pdf) | ISBN 9781681516646 (library binding) | ISBN
  9781681524504 (pbk.)
Subjects: LCSH: Rapinoe, Megan,--Juvenile literature. | Women soccer
  players--United States--Biography--Juvenile literature. | Soccer
  players--United States--Biography--Juvenile literature.
Classification: LCC GV942.7.R366 (ebook) | LCC GV942.7.R366 S54 2020
(print) | DDC 796.334092 [2] --dc23
LC record available at https://lccn.loc.gov/2018038007

Photo Credits: AP/Jack Dempsey cover; AP/Robin Alam, Icon Sportswire 2;
Alamy/Juan Lainez, Marin Media, Cal Sport Media 4–5; Alamy/
Paul Kitagaki Jr., Sacramento Bee, Zuma Press 6–7;
Getty/Darren Abate, Stringer 8; Newscom/Robin Alam,
Icon SMI 11; AP/David Klein, Sportimage, Cal Sport Media 12;
Alamy/Thomas Eisenhuth, dpa picture alliance
archive 15; Getty/Joern Pollex, FIFA 16; Getty/Beck
Starr, WireImage 19; AP/Diego Diaz, Icon
Sportswire 20–21; WikiCommons/Pierre-Yves
Beaudouin 22

Editor: Alissa Thielges
Designer: Aubrey Harper
Photo Researcher: Holly Young

Printed in the United States of America

HC 10 9 8 7 6 5 4 3 2 1
PB 10 9 8 7 6 5 4 3 2 1

TABLE OF CONTENTS

4

HERE COMES MEGAN

A player zips down the field. She has
the ball. That's Megan Rapinoe! She
is sneaky. She kicks. Goal! Rapinoe
always finds a way to score. She is a
skilled soccer player.

FAMILY SUPPORT

Rapinoe started playing soccer at age three. Her dad coached her youth soccer games. Her family watches every pro game. They are her biggest fans.

ON THE FIELD

Rapinoe played soccer in college. She was a **midfielder**. This position helps to defend the goal. She also helped her team score. Rapinoe did it all.

Rapinoe is two-footed. She can kick with either foot.

GOING PRO

Rapinoe has a lot of **passion**. She gives each game her all. In 2009, she was **drafted** into the pros. The Chicago Red Stars chose her for their team.

GLOBETROTTER

In 2011, Rapinoe began playing abroad. She was on teams in Australia and France. They call the sport **futbol**.

Rapinoe is also on the U.S. national team. She is a forward.

THE WORLD CUP

In 2011, Rapinoe made an incredible play during the Women's World Cup tournament. She and her teammate, Abby Wambach (number 20), made a last second goal to tie the game. It's the latest goal ever scored in a World Cup match.

TEAM USA

Rapinoe played at the 2012 Olympics. She scored two goals in a **semifinal** match. Not many have done this. Rapinoe helped Team USA bring home the gold.

Rapinoe was injured at the 2016 Olympics. She only played in the first round of games.

ATHLETE ALLY

Rapinoe came out as a lesbian in 2012. She knows it can be hard for gay athletes to be themselves. She works to help them feel more included in sports.

One percent of Rapinoe's salary goes to soccer charities that help gay athletes.

Gay & Lesbian Center

19

20

SOCCER STAR

Rapinoe now plays for the Seattle Reign FC. She is a top scorer. In 2018, she won an ESPY for Best National Women's Soccer League Player. This was a new award. She was the first to win it.

JUST THE FACTS

Born: July 5, 1985

Hometown: Redding, California

College: University of Portland

International debut: 2011

Teams: U.S. Women's National Team; Seattle Reign FC

Position: Forward

Accomplishments:

- ESPY Award for Best NWSL Player: 2018

- Women's World Cup: 2015 (gold), 2011 (silver)

- Algarve Cup: 2013, Player of the Tournament

- Olympic Gold: 2012

- ESPY Award for Play of the Year: 2011

WORDS TO KNOW

drafted – selected by a team

forward – a player who is responsible for most of a team's scoring

futbol – what some countries call soccer

midfielder – a player positioned in the middle of the field to assist defense and offense

passion – a very strong feeling, such as love, for something

semifinal – the series of games that decide who will play in the final game

LEARN MORE

Read More

Ignotofsky, Rachel. *Women in Sports: 50 Fearless Athletes Who Played to Win*. New York: Ten Speed Press, 2017.

Nagelhout, Ryan. *Abby Wambach*. New York: Garreth Stevens Publishing, 2017.

Savage, Jeff. *US Women's National Team: Soccer Champions*. Minneapolis: Lerner Publications, 2018.

Websites

Official Website of Megan Rapinoe
www.rapinoe.us

U.S. Soccer: Megan Rapinoe
www.ussoccer.com/players/r/megan-rapinoe#tab-1

INDEX

Every effort has been made to ensure that these websites are appropriate for children. However, because of the nature of the Internet, it is impossible to guarantee that these sites will remain active indefinitely or that their contents will not be altered.